TIME FOR KIDS READERS

Doctors Without Borders

by Heather Miller

Harcourt

Orlando   Austin   Chicago   New York   Toronto   London   San Diego

Visit *The Learning Site!*
www.harcourtschool.com

Most people in the United States just pick up the phone and call a doctor if they're not feeling well. Or they go to a nearby clinic. For them, medical help is never far away. But it isn't like that everywhere in the world.

What happens to people who have no local doctors to help them? What happens to people who don't live near hospitals? Whom can they turn to in an emergency? They might turn to Doctors Without Borders.

Doctors Without Borders is a group of doctors, nurses, and other volunteers. They donate their efforts and their time. They take medical treatment, food, medicine, and emergency supplies to people in many parts of the world. They travel to areas that have been damaged by wars or natural disasters.

The doctors and nurses of Doctors Without Borders go where other doctors and nurses cannot—or will not—go. Sometimes they are in great danger. They go into war zones, where they risk being shot at. They care for people who have serious illnesses. Often, the doctors and nurses must work in very isolated and primitive parts of the world. They travel to jungles and deserts and into rugged mountains to take care of people who are ill.

Near Iraq, a Kurdish mother thanks a volunteer nurse, Reinardt Byl. He wears a T-shirt that identifies his group, Doctors Without Borders.

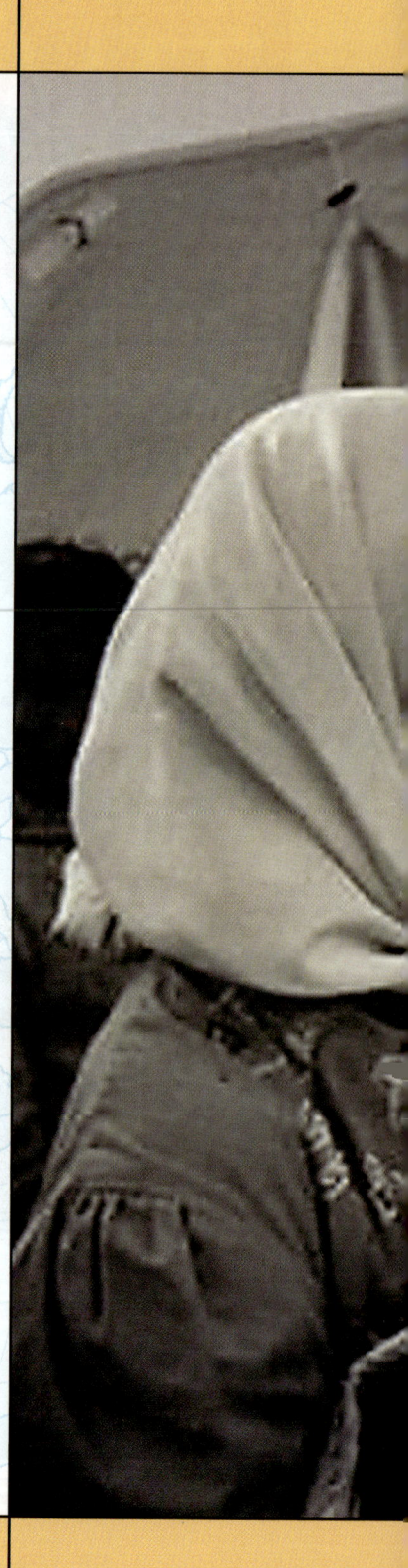

Countries all over the world welcome Doctors Without Borders because its volunteers stay neutral. They do not take sides in any conflicts taking place in the countries they serve. They help people no matter who they are or what they believe.

Doctors Without Borders receives funds from many sources. It depends on donations from ordinary people around the world. Support also comes from businesses and other organizations that want to help. Governments help out, too, though the group does not accept money from nations that are involved in conflicts.

Doctors Without Borders was created because of the suffering that a French doctor, Bernard Kouchner (koosh•NEHR), saw in Africa. In 1967, a civil war broke out in Nigeria (ny•JIR•ee•uh), a West African country. One part of the country tried to break away and form a new country named Biafra (bee•AHF•ruh). The civil war dragged on for three years, and many people were killed or badly hurt.

Dr. Bernard Kouchner unloads sacks of rice.

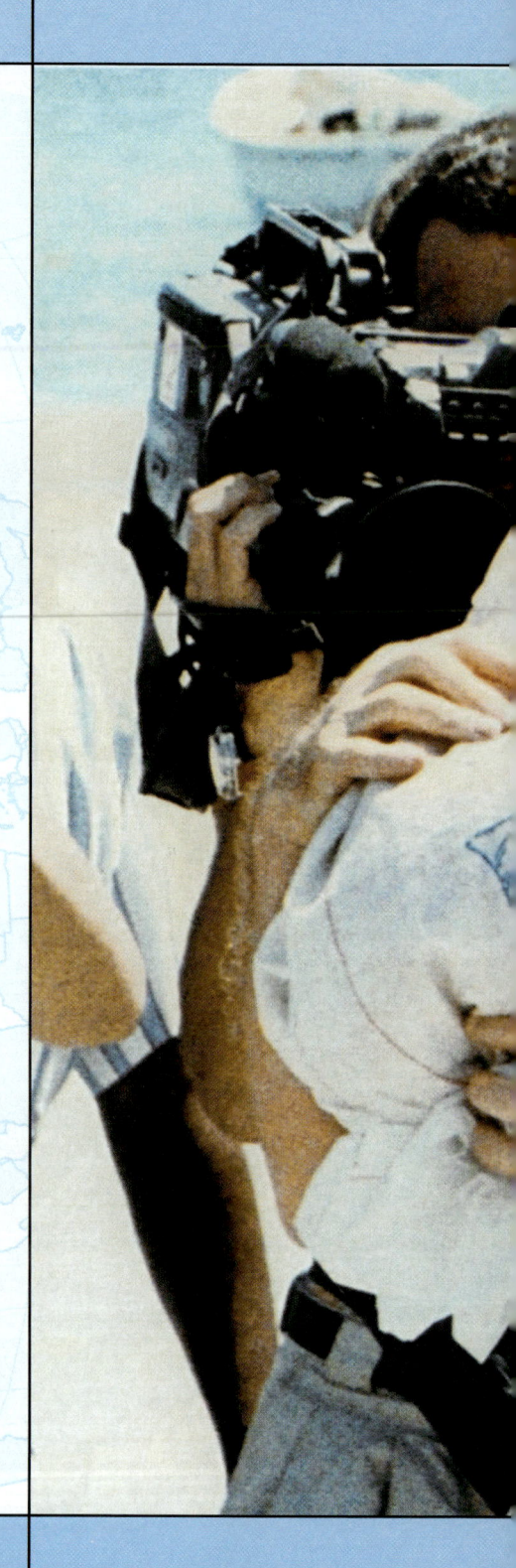

4

5

AFRICA

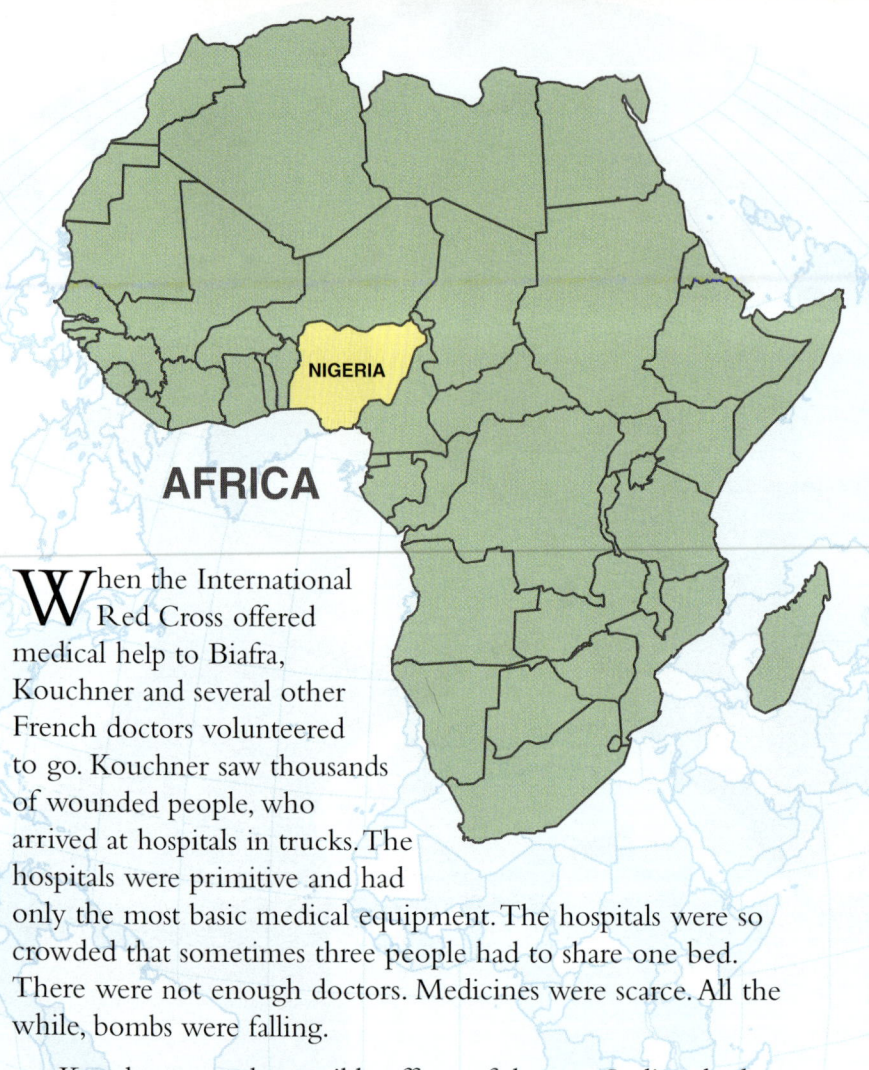

NIGERIA

When the International Red Cross offered medical help to Biafra, Kouchner and several other French doctors volunteered to go. Kouchner saw thousands of wounded people, who arrived at hospitals in trucks. The hospitals were primitive and had only the most basic medical equipment. The hospitals were so crowded that sometimes three people had to share one bed. There were not enough doctors. Medicines were scarce. All the while, bombs were falling.

Kouchner saw the terrible effects of the war. It disturbed him, and the memories of it stayed with him. When he returned to France in 1969, he spoke and wrote about the need for more international medical help. He wanted to do more. During the months that followed, Kouchner returned twice to Africa to work. He decided he had to do even more. In 1970, he joined with other doctors to form the Emergency Medical and Surgical Intervention Group. This group provided care for people during emergencies and in times of disaster.

At a refugee camp in Nigeria, women and children receive food.

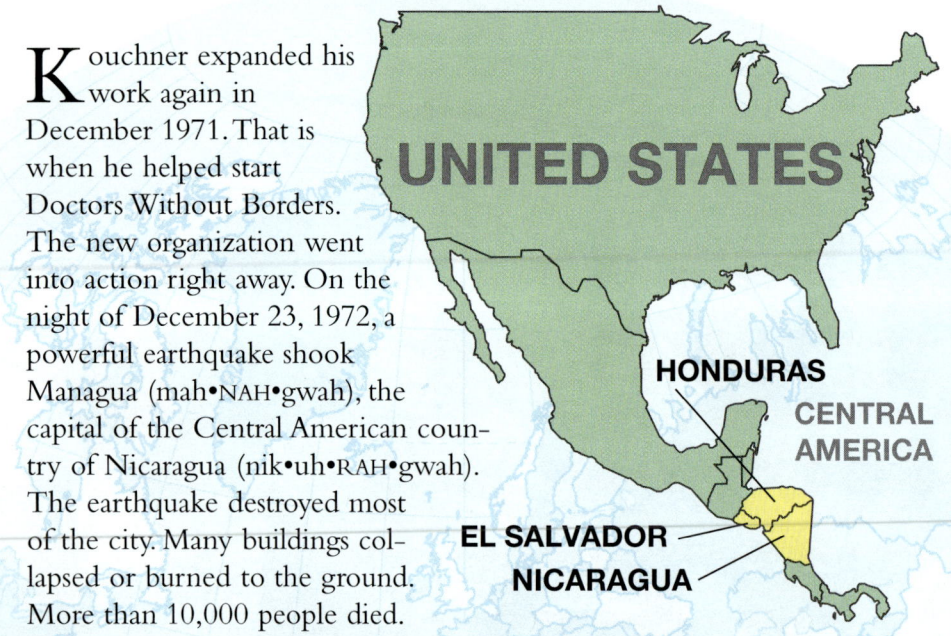

Kouchner expanded his work again in December 1971. That is when he helped start Doctors Without Borders. The new organization went into action right away. On the night of December 23, 1972, a powerful earthquake shook Managua (mah•NAH•gwah), the capital of the Central American country of Nicaragua (nik•uh•RAH•gwah). The earthquake destroyed most of the city. Many buildings collapsed or burned to the ground. More than 10,000 people died. Thousands of other people were left injured and homeless. In September 1974, Hurricane Fifi struck Honduras (hahn•DUR•uhs), another country in Central America. The hurricane killed more than 8,000 people and injured thousands of others. It destroyed homes, schools, and hospitals. Doctors Without Borders brought medical aid to help the victims of both disasters.

Doctors Without Borders is still working hard more than 30 years later. In January 2001, another big earthquake rocked Central America. In the small country of El Salvador (el SAL•vuh•dawr), the quake started a landslide that buried hundreds of homes. In February, just one month later, another earthquake killed 315 people and injured more than 3,000 others. Doctors Without Borders was there once again to help provide medical aid.

Natural disasters such as earthquakes and hurricanes are a special challenge for Doctors Without Borders. Help has to come fast—or people die. Doctors Without Borders stores medical supplies and equipment in its warehouses. Volunteers are ready to fly into a disaster area right away to treat the injured. In emergencies, doctors do surgery under the most difficult conditions. Sometimes there is no electricity. Doctors might perform operations with the headlights of a car to light the area.

In El Salvador, a man walks past the rubble of houses destroyed by an earthquake.

TFK IT'S A FACT

Doctors Without Borders Time Line

1972	Nicaragua
1974	Honduras
1976	Lebanon
1979	Afghanistan
1980	Somalia
1985	El Salvador
1988	Armenia
1989	Eastern Europe
1992	Somalia
1993–1995	Burundi
1996	Nigeria
1998–1999	Kosovo and East Timor
2000	Ethiopia
2001	Afghanistan

Children at a refugee camp in Ethiopia surround a Doctors Without Borders volunteer who has brought them medical supplies.

Often there are other problems—such as dirty or diseased water, or wrecked roads and hospitals. At a disaster site, Doctors Without Borders gives out clean drinking water and food. Its volunteers dig new wells and bring in truckloads of supplies to build sewage systems. They also restore hospitals and clinics to working condition. When they find people who are starving, they bring in food and teach nutrition programs. If necessary, Doctors Without Borders sends in engineers to help rebuild water systems or important roads.

In their work, Doctors Without Borders volunteers often see the realities of war. They see the suffering of the people they help. This often changes the way the volunteers think. Many of them return to their home countries with a different understanding. They cannot ignore suffering in any part of the world. Many volunteers work for change in their home countries. They also work to change the living conditions of the people they cared for far away.

Some volunteers protest unjust laws on behalf of people who have no voice in their government. Doctors Without Borders has brought its concerns before the United Nations. The organization also seeks support for its point of view from the press—in newspapers, on radio, and on television.

When an earthquake knocked down her home, Doctors Without Borders gave this woman cooking supplies, such as pots.

TFK BY THE NUMBERS

4	Number of weeks' notice most Doctors Without Borders (DWB) volunteers get before a mission
6	Months most doctors and nurses stay on an assignment
80	Number of countries in which DWB works
700	Monthly salary in dollars of most new volunteers
1,000	Number of health care workers DWB trains each year
2,500	Number of volunteers who work for DWB each year

RUSSIA

CHECHNYA

GEORGIA

TURKEY ARMENIA

During the past few years, Doctors Without Borders volunteers have stood up for the people of Chechnya (CHECH•ny•uh). Chechnya is a small region of Russia. In 1991, it wanted to become independent. When Russia tried to hold on to Chechnya, a war erupted. By the time the war officially ended in the spring of 2000, thousands of people had been hurt or killed. Volunteers for Doctors Without Borders saw many people badly treated during the war and brought that information to the rest of the world.

Doctors Without Borders volunteers also spoke out about the cruelty they saw in Angola (ang•GOH•luh), a country in southern Africa. The people of Angola had been fighting a civil war for many years. Volunteers from Doctors Without Borders saw soldiers torture many people. The soldiers also forced more than 2.5 million people out of their homes. These people became refugees. The volunteers helped the sick in Angola. They also told the world about the brutality they saw there.

Children at a camp for Chechen refugees do their best to stay neat and clean.

Doctors Without Borders works to stop conflicts, because the group knows that war can do great damage. It sponsors programs to help people understand how hard it is for children to grow up in a place where there is always fighting. The group hopes that this information will make people work harder to avoid war. The group also helps people learn about the damage war does to food supplies and how war creates homelessness and starvation. The doctors hope to help people to choose peace instead of war.

Doctors Without Borders also helps people with mental problems caused by war and terrorism. Doctors Without Borders began its first mental-health program in 1991. Since then, mental-health care has become an important part of its emergency projects. For example, during times of drought, when there is no rain and the land dries up, hunger and thirst increase not only physical but mental suffering. If people do not get help, their problems can become worse. As a result, victims and their families can have trouble starting their lives over.

In 1999, Doctors Without Borders received the Nobel Peace Prize. The award usually goes to individuals, such as Dr. Martin Luther King, Jr., the American civil rights leader, and Nelson Mandela, the South African leader. Only four organizations have won or shared the award in the past 20 years.

Dr. Kouchner once said, "Mankind's suffering belongs to all people." The workers of Doctors Without Borders believe this strongly. In times of war and disaster, their mission to help all the people who need them continues.

Children illustrate one of the goals of Doctors Without Borders—peace.

TFK Spotlight

Dr. Bernard Kouchner was born in France on November 1, 1939. When he was growing up, Kouchner wanted to become a journalist. However, he decided to follow in the footsteps of his father and become a doctor.

Kouchner helped found Doctors Without Borders in 1971. He worked with the group for several years. Kouchner wanted his group to take a more active role with respect to war and suffering. At the time, many of the leaders of Doctors Without Borders felt uncomfortable with this position. So Kouchner left Doctors Without Borders in 1979. He started another organization, called Doctors of the World. This group also takes care of victims of wars and natural disasters.

Kouchner worked with Doctors of the World for a while. In 1999, he became a special representative at the United Nations. Then the government of France asked him to become the Minister of Health. Although Kouchner no longer works with Doctors Without Borders, he still supports its ideals. He also continues to speak out about injustice. The great South African leader Nelson Mandela once told Kouchner, "Thank you for interfering in things that do not concern you." Kouchner intends to keep interfering.

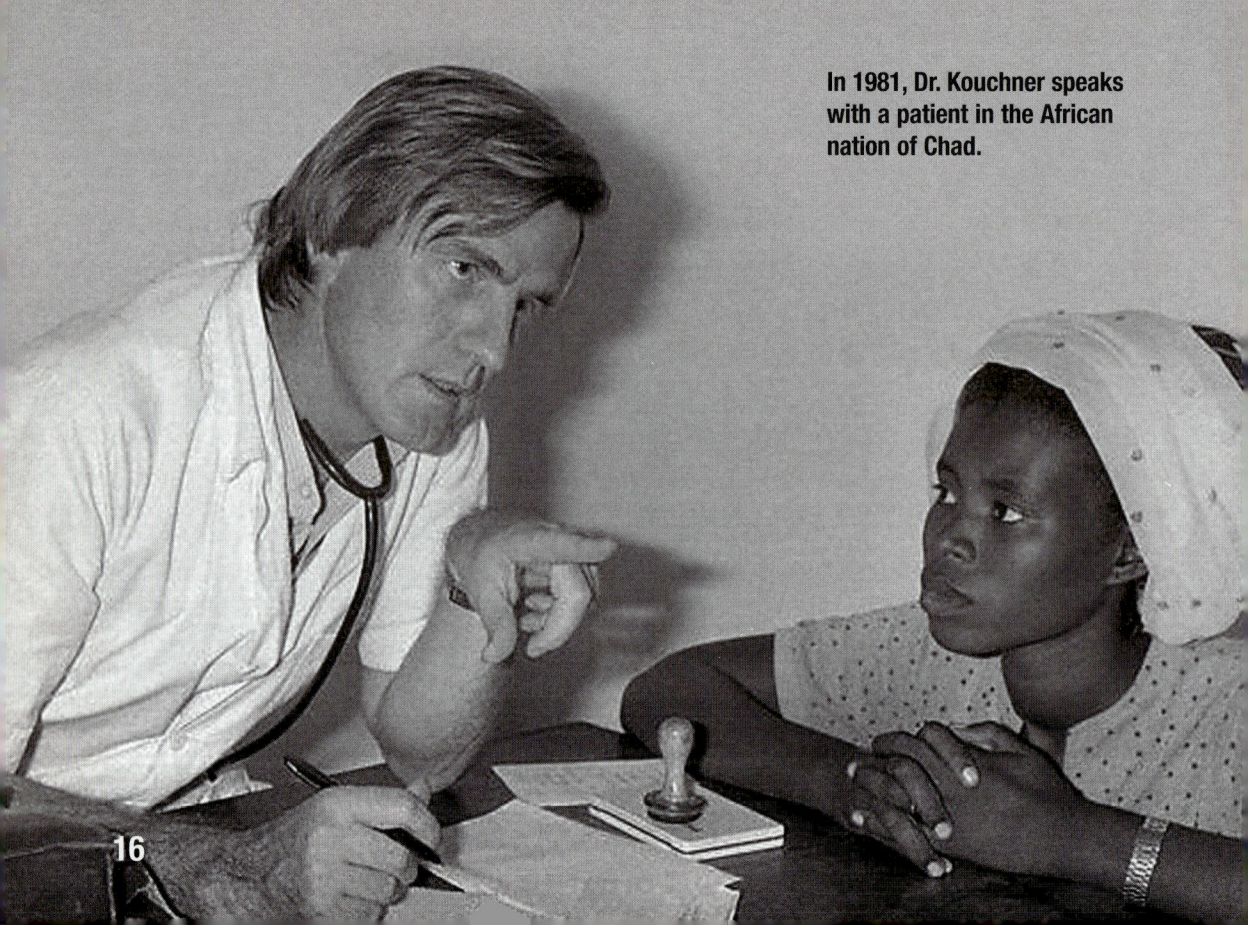

In 1981, Dr. Kouchner speaks with a patient in the African nation of Chad.